Healing Infidelity In Marriages

Eight (8) Powerful Secrets
For Wives
Learned From The Other Woman:
An Uncommon Guide To
Fortify Your Marriage

Research Allows Cheating
Husbands To Tell All

By: Deciann Richards

Copyright Page

All rights reserved. No part of this book may be reproduced, distributed or transmitted in any form or by any means including photocopying, recording, electronic or mechanical methods without the permission of the author and publisher except in the case of brief quotations embodied in critical reviews and certain other non-commercial uses permitted by copyright law.

Please note that the author reserves the right to revise or adjust any information found in this book, so as to improve the accuracy of its contents.

Copyright © 2019 Deciann Richards
All rights reserved.
ISBN: 978-1-7108-3231-0

Self-published in Kingston, Jamaica

Editing & Proof-Reading: Ms. Kerri-Ann Sawyers and Mrs. Henry McDonald

Book Cover Photographer: Mr. Norman Wallace Jr.

Legal Disclaimer

The information found in this book is based on a research that was completed by the author. The author is not at all responsible for the utilization of any strategy or suggestion found in this book. The author does not take any responsibility whatsoever for any injury or harm that may occur by the reader because he or she utilized the suggestions or information found in this book

This publication is designed to provide competent and reliable information regarding the subject matter covered. However, it is sold with the understanding that the author and publisher are not engaged in rendering legal, psychological or other professional advice. If legal or expert service is required, a professional should be sought. You may use the strategies and suggestions found in this book at your own risk.

Research Limitations

The actual questionnaire used in this research can be found in the appendix section of this book.

The research conducted was limited to infidelities committed by men with women.

The researcher did not use any program to analyse the data collected. Data collected was analysed by the researcher herself.

Based on the instructions and guidelines affixed to the questionnaire, the researcher presumes that all respondents were men and were aware of the intended purpose of the information being collected.

*Please Visit My Website to
Receive Your Free Workbook on
'How to Heal Infidelity in Your Marriage'*

www.deciannrichards.com

Content

Thank You   Page 8

Why Did I Write This Book?   Page 10

Introduction   Page 14

Can You Handle the Truth?   Page 19

Secret #1   Page 46

Secret #2   Page 61

Secret #3   Page 88

Secret #4   Page 105

Secret #5   Page 136

Secret #6   Page 145

Secret #7   Page 153

Secret # 8   Page 164

Thank You

All praise to my Lord and personal Savior, Jesus Christ who has endowed me with the inspiration and the mind to take on this challenge. To speak so openly and candidly about this subject matter.

Secondly, thanks to all the participants who completed my questionnaire. Thank you for speaking so honestly about this very sacred issue.

To my husband, Steve Nathaniel Richards who has taught me so many of life's gems. Who has challenged my timidity and has taught me to be fearless and resilient, refusing to accept any closed door that I may want to see open.

To my son Elijah in the words of Frankie Valli, "My Eyes Adored You" (Valli, 1975). From the minute I laid eyes on you, I loved you. From the day you winked your little eyes at me in that hospital room, you became in sync with the beat of my heart.

To my mother Norma Campbell, my sisters Jacqueline Trowers and Pamella Hibbert you all have invested your time, love and energy in helping me to become the woman I am today.

Thank You & Love Always

Why Did I Write This Book?

The journey of this book started one day when breaking news that a married Jamaica Defense Force soldier was found dead in a motel bathroom in Spanish Town. Reports are that this soldier went out to drink and have a good time at a nearby bar. While drinking and having a good time, he consumed several alcoholic beverages and a sexual enhancement pill. After this, he rented a motel room to have sex with a female companion, fell ill, and eventually dropped dead in his infidelities. The release of his naked dead picture in his motel bathroom stormed through various social media platforms and caught the attention of thousands across the world.

The release of this news left an indelible mark on me as a married woman who at the time had been married for almost fifteen (15) years. The questions regarding his infidelity and his final moments unfolded in my mind.

As these thoughts unfolded, they produced pertinent questions in my heart. After hearing of this man's plight, I got up that morning, and for me, it could not be business as usual. I had to spend some time talking with my husband just having a genuine heart to heart conversation with him regarding this incident. As the conversation unfolded, I began to ask my husband some of these questions. As these questions began to project from me, a quest unfolded before my eyes – a quest which led me on a journey in search of specific knowledge regarding infidelity and the other woman.

As this search for knowledge began to grow inside of me, I realized that I didn't want these questions to be answered through hypothesis or the opinions of others. But I wanted these answers to come directly from the men who had committed infidelities. Married men who would be brave and honest enough to tell me the truth about the temptation to commit infidelity. The issues that led them to commit infidelity (for those who would admit this) and their relationship with the other woman.

I desired to equip every wife with the secrets needed to fortify and heal infidelity in their marriage. The truth for every wife is that we may not know if our husbands have committed infidelity; we may not know if our husbands are committing infidelity. However, we know that the possibility of the other woman in our relationship is very real! The world of infidelity and the dynamics of this other relationship became my new quest! However, to know the absolute truth I needed to invade the hearts and minds of men who were willing to admit to me, whether or not they had committed infidelity and the reason/s that triggered and perpetuated this decision. Hence, to get the truth regarding the issue at hand, fifty (50) married and separated men were randomly selected to anonymously complete questionnaires regarding infidelity in their own marriage/s. Fifty (50) married and separated women were also asked to complete questionnaires as well.

The responses derived from these questionnaires were analyzed and used to create the *Eight (8) Powerful Secrets For Wives Learned From The Other Woman: An Uncommon Guide To Fortify Your Marriage*. Therefore, most of the information highlighted in this book is not solely the opinions of the author. The secrets found in this book are mainly the views, ideas and confessions of men and women who completed these questionnaires.

Introduction

Confronting and speaking about infidelity within marriages has become an issue met with much taboo and hypocrisy. In today's society and the era in which we live, events of infidelity have become a much more likely phenomenon in many marital relationships. However, only a few couples will speak about this issue, much less to openly and honestly confront it. Within the dynamics of every sexually committed relationship, the possibility of infidelity is a real event that every couple must confront and address.

Ironically, infidelity has raised its ugly head in many social and structural settings. It has transcended the barriers of social-economic class, race, gender and even religion. It has made its entrance into homes, religious arenas, the white house, political campaign trails and organizations, and its effects in many marriages are undeniable.

For years, I have had a deep concern for marriages, seeing that I myself have been married for over fifteen (15) years. In my attempt to solidify my own marriage and give it the fighting chance that it so rightly deserves, I also had to confront the issue of *'Infidelity'* and this concept of *'The Other Woman'*. Hence, this book is for a mature woman who is willing to lay aside the plethora of her emotional basket, to gain great wisdom and a deeper insight into the hooks, strategies and operations of *'The Other Woman'*.

If as couples, we intend to sincerely live happy and fulfilling marriages, we must now be willing to closely examine the dynamics of *'infidelity'*. Deeply embedded within this dynamic is a crucial and noteworthy element called *'The*

Other Woman'. For a lot of wives, this conversation regarding 'her' is often met with feelings of great offense and personal inadequacies. However, I believe that one of the key elements in confronting and addressing this issue is to closely examine the operations of *'this woman'*. To investigate her hooks, strategies and to carefully examine the table she prepares and spreads for husbands.

It is a fact that *you cannot fight an enemy that you don't understand.* As wives, we must realize that an integral part of success in any marriage is a key component called *'knowledge'*. Hence, it is of utmost importance that we are *duly informed* and *schooled*, even from the most *unconventional places*. Here, it's learning *secrets from 'The Other Woman'*.

Let me make this unequivocally clear, *I am not glorifying the concept of this 'The Other Woman'*. However, it is my *sincere intention* to *empower, equip and duly inform* every wife about the strategies, hooks and offerings of these side chicks. In so doing I intend to expose the secret weapons and empires created by these ladies. Neither am I suggesting that the actions or inactions of wives are the main reasons for infidelity or failed marriages. However, based on my research and discussions with men, I am suggesting that the ideas found in this book, are noteworthy of every wife in examining this matter more closely. Even the good book admonishes us by saying 'My people are destroyed for lack of knowledge' (Hosea 4: 6, King James Version) It further states that we should not let the enemy outsmart us because we are not ignorant of his devises (2 Corinthians 2:11, New Living Translation)

Finally, please note that the ideas and principles highlighted in this book are not meant to be a broad-brush advice for every wife. These strategies and ideologies are not guaranteed to stop any case of infidelity. However, if as couples we intent to truly live healthy, happy and fulfilling marriages, then we must begin this discussion with our spouses. We must honestly examine *'the man in the mirror'*. We must be willing to examine ourselves in light of the discussion found in this book. We must be honest enough to examine our *weaknesses and strengths* to fortify our marriages, making them stronger and better.

Can You Really Handle the Truth?

Many wives say I wish he had told me the truth. It's not the infidelity that makes me so furiously angry, it was the *'lie.'* A *secured 'lie'* that was hidden in the vault of his actions and demeanor. Many wives say this after discovering that infidelity has crept into the marriage. Some wives are even adamant that the revelation of this truth at a very early stage would have changed their feelings and response to the whole issue at hand. While I understand the arguments presented by these wives, I also know an alternate truth, which presents itself alongside this adamant demand. This is deeply embedded in the question of *'Can You Really Handle the Truth?'* The response to this lingering question prevents some husbands from speaking the truth. The truth of the matter is that most men know that there are consequences at the revelation of their indiscretion. They are fully aware that their actions will bring certain ramifications. Hence, it is not the initial series of reasonable backlash from their wives that prevent them from telling the truth. It is the *'life sentence'* that some men may receive from telling such truth.

One husband said to his wife after confessing to her that he had committed infidelity, now had a child outside the marriage and was trying to recommit himself to the marital relationship.

He said:

'You never questioned me; you never asked me questions before. When I was having sex with other women, you never asked. And now after confessing and trying to work on myself and the relationship. I am badgered with questions and suspicion.' (paraphrasing)

This story conveyed to me by his wife is the real concern for some men.

We've also heard of more emasculating stories where women turn up at workplaces and other social spaces, and completely embarrass their spouses after finding out about their indiscretions. These are just a few of the gnawing and real concerns for some married men.

Other concerns may include:
- The continuous attack on his character
- The unending mountains of suspicion and mistrust
- The endless torture of questions

- The emasculating of his manhood in front of friends, family, neighbors, coworkers, associates and whosoever will listen.

It is true that some husbands not wanting to tell the truth, has nothing to do with the fear of these repercussions. It has nothing to do with the reasonable backlash from their wives. Some husbands do not want to tell the truth and have no intentions of telling the truth because they do not intend to truly commit to the marital relationship. Their true goal is to stay married while maintaining a sexual relationship with the other woman.

Research for this book has revealed that twenty three percent (23%) of men admit that they prefer to stay married while maintaining a sexual relationship with the other woman. On the other hand, thirty-four percent (34%) say they have never committed infidelity. While sixty-five percent (65%) of men who admit to having an extra-marital affair express a willingness to recommit to the marital relationship. The statistics highlighted above may not be encouraging or impressive for some wives. However, the truth of the matter is that there is a percentage of men who are committed and others who have a desire to recommit to the marital relationship.

If this morning when you were about to leave home, the meteorologist said that there is a sixty five percent (65%) probability that rain will fall, would you think of walking with your umbrella? You probably would! Just the possibility, the real possibility of an event occurring, often cause people to react. In Jamaica and all over the world, people invest sure money for probable winnings. The lottery has become a daily habit for some people all over the world. Why? Because of its great potential, because of the magnitude of the potential win.

The reality is that some husbands express a willingness to recommit to the marital relationship; if it is fed with the nutrients needed for it to thrive, allowing it to become more dynamic, joyous, exciting and healthy. This sincere intention and an honest willingness to recommit to the relationship should be a noteworthy indicator to wives. The fact is that there are some marital relationships where infidelity has crept in, raised its ugly head and husbands are no longer willing to work on these relationships.

For a husband to sincerely show his willingness to recommit, this is undeniably a very crucial ingredient needed to restore the marriage and heal infidelity. This is possibly one of the most important ingredients needed in restoring any marriage. Just ask every wife who dug deep, extended her arms of forgiveness and willingness, but received a shut door from her husband. A wife willing to try, but her husband turned his back and walked straight through the door.

The truth is, marriage is a great investment that must be nurtured through sweat, tears and effort (pure hard work). The feeling of accomplishment, victory and the overcoming of great obstacles together as a couple is a priceless reward that will bring to most couples the feeling of a million-dollar winning.

Hence, for the prize or demise that is at stake, as wives and even as husbands we must dig a little deeper, drill a bit longer and toil a little extra for the sweet taste of the probable winnings that are ahead.

What's in His Soul?

Telling the absolute truth is not as easy as you believe. If you are honest with yourself, telling the whole truth requires great courage, which is an acquired taste for most people. Just like the taste of Broccoli, Brussels Sprouts, Celery Sticks and even Spinach. Developing the ability to consume and appreciate *'the absolute truth'* is a process that becomes easier after much exposure.

For any man to acquire the taste of *'truth-telling'*, he must be willing and courageous enough to confront the truth. That is seeing the truth, acknowledging that what he sees is the truth, and accepting what he sees. For some men, this is a very difficult process. Hence, the creation of an alternate world consisting of *'his truths and realities'*.

It is not that he is unaware of what he is doing and some of what is happening. It is that he may not have fully processed the whole scenario that is unfolding. He may not have spent time coming to full awareness with his choices, the magnitude of the situation and its full effects. He is on autopilot going through the motion, enjoying the momentary pleasures available to him. He has not spent the time fully reflecting on the truth about his situation and the 'man in the mirror'.

And even if he has processed the truth, the whole truth, the reality of this truth may be immensely difficult for him to deal with, much more to admit these truths to his wife.

Maybe the truth is:

- He feels like he doesn't love his wife anymore, or maybe the love that he had for her has significantly decreased.
- He no longer finds his wife attractive, sexy or an object of his sexual fantasy.
- He is tired of the routine relationship that he has with his wife.
- He wants something different. He wants to feel something different. [mmm]
- His wife doesn't give him the affection and attention that he desires.
- He didn't love his wife in the first place. He only got married to her because she was pregnant or he felt he had to at the time.

- He changed his mind; he doesn't want to be married anymore. [shhhh]

How easy is it, for a man to process these realities and be entirely honest with himself? How does he convey to his wife these truths, the absolute truth about his new feelings? Barring none, this is a difficult process for him and sometimes, instead of choosing the painful option of telling his wife the truth, he seeks the alternative avenue of having his needs met by 'The Other Woman'.

Sometimes, when a man, a married man sees value in his marital relationship, when he has a degree of care for his wife's feelings and her emotional state, he will bypass telling her the truth in an attempt to avoid hurting her feelings. Hence his alternative solution, in finding relief in 'the other woman', 'in his mind', 'in his world', everyone is happy at the moment. He can cope a little better with his "nagging" wife, he can numb the truth about his unsettling feelings and he can show up to perform his expected duties both at home and at work. The home is well kept, things are running efficiently, the children are happy and all is well. Everything is seemingly okay at home. He is doing well at work, and he gets that little extra twenty percent (20%) elsewhere. This solution for him at the moment feels like a good idea. To him, it is the band-aid that covers and hides the reality of the present truth, in an attempt to arrive at a momentary place of happiness.

I know that this situation may be completely difficult for some wives to understand. However, this is the untold truth for some married men. **Hence, learning to create an environment of truth is an essential craft that all wives**

should learn to master.

Learning to Create an Environment of Truth

In learning to create an environment of truth, your response to any degree of truth is crucial. Suppose you had a friend, who had a severe problem that he or she wanted to speak to you about? Even if your friend went ahead, set the time and date to have lunch to share these issues with you, I want you to be sure that your friend more than likely, would have been a little apprehensive about sharing. He or she might have tussled with the idea of canceling the lunch date or even giving you a flimsy excuse to avoid the discussion altogether.

Now imagine that this friend is your husband, yes, that same husband who may be sitting beside you in the living room while you're reading this book. Imagine that he has been struggling with infidelity and a host of other related issues. Maybe he has been having a sexual relationship with another woman. However, he now recognizes his mistakes and is ready to confess and recommit himself to the marital relationship.

Without a shadow of a doubt, your response to this situation is crucial to the degree of truth that he will tell you now, and in the future. If at the bearing of his soul, you begin to through a violent tantrum, then more than likely you will not be privy to the complete truth. If at the beginning of telling the truth, you begin to behave very irrational and violently emotional, then the degree of truth that he will tell you may be compromised.

I completely understand that this event is a painful scenario that you would have preferred avoiding. However, this maybe the medicine that your relationship needs in order to heal.

When the truth is being presented to you, try to remain objective and rational. Seeing that this may be a great opportunity for you to hear *'the absolute truth'*. May be this is the first time that you will hear the absolute truth, and realize the magnitude of the situation at hand. Hence, remain as calm and objective as possible. Listen to him and allow him to tell you everything. The redemption that you desire maybe found somewhere in what he is saying to you. The only way for you to really hear the truth, the absolute truth is to listen to him! Now based on the amount of information that he will give to you; you will now have a better idea of what is really happening.

Listening

When you are listening to your husband, rambling or mumbling out some truth, do not become conceited or too emotional while listening; again, try to remain objective, civil and as calm as possible, so you will hear the truth, the way it is presented to you.

As I carefully advise you from a place of love, do not for a minute believe that I am only giving advice from the position of a novice. That thinking is far from the truth. I have had to sit in the seat of my own advice at some points in my marriage, where the discussion unfolding was not what I wanted to hear from my husband. However, my ability to remain calm, less emotional, more objective, clear-headed and logical is what gave me the edge to later on in my marriage reap maybe not all truths, but some degree of bareback truth about the issues confronting us.

Not that I have never thrown a fit! But the more I became exposed to the truth in my marriage, the more I have learned to remain calm and a bit more level-headed; not falling prey to my raging emotions at all times. The human fact is this, once you have formed a habit of exposing yourself to the truth, then hearing, processing and receiving the truth becomes a little easier. I have learned a simple truth about life; when you make it a habit of telling yourself the truth, you develop the craft and skills needed in processing the truth without always becoming offended. Hence, truth processing becomes a little easier. As wives, I believe that some of us have not made 'complete truth processing' a habitual part of our internal compass. As the saying goes, 'If you lie to the world, do not lie to yourself, tell yourself the truth'. We are all guilty at times of not telling ourselves the absolute truth. Hence when we hear the complete truth, its impact is exceedingly devastating to our internal compass, because we have created a glasshouse in which to live. The truth has the potential to strengthen us and make us stronger and healthier. As the good book says, 'Judge yourself, that others will not need to judge you' (1 Corinthians 11: 31, New American Standard Bible). Learn to analyze your strengths & weaknesses. You will become more aware and conscious of potential issues that may be lingering in your marriage. Once you know these potential issues, this improves your ability to take action.

If we make it a habit to tell ourselves the truth, the whole truth and nothing but the truth, then as wives we will become more prone to think logically, objectively and rationally even during emotionally challenging times.

Being Responsible with the Truth

If you want your partner to fully expose himself to you, you must prove to yourself that you can be entirely responsible with the truth. I understand that 'the truth' can be extremely challenging and painful. But your ability to be responsible with it, is paramount to the degree of healing that will take place. Healing here does not only mean staying in the relationship. Even if there is to be a separation, the lives involved in this situation will be able to heal and recover faster when the truth is handled responsibly.

In Being Responsible with the Truth, You Need to Understand a Few Things:

There are marriages that have been healed and fully restored after infidelity. Hence, the exposure of your most intimate affairs must be handled delicately and with the utmost care. In that, you must be conscious of who you choose to confide in, and what you say.

Do not air the sacredness of your most intimate affairs in the public domain. You, your husband, your children, your church community and extended family, will be tried in the court of public opinion. Believe me, if you do this, you will add to your life a deep ocean of regrets, pressure and stress. If you choose to tell others let it be when the situation has come to a resolve and the healing process is completed. When you have spent sufficient time with yourself, deliberating and carefully deciding. After you've had time, to accept and become comfortable with the decision that you've made regarding the direction of your marriage.

If you have a large social network, it is not wise to tell all your friends. This sensitive information must be handled with the utmost care and respect. Hence, only a few of your most confidential, mature and responsible friends, must be entrusted with this intimate knowledge about your relationship. Trust me on this, a man can cope with a lot of things. He can cope with your crying (bawling), your tantrums and maybe a few hits given to him out of your complete hurt, anger and disappointment (behind closed doors). However, if you emasculate him in front of your friends, family members, neighbors, children and coworkers, the potential for healing and restoration of your marriage will be difficult.

Keep this in an extremely small circle of mature, unbiased friends who are responsible, and are able to offer emotional, mental and spiritual support. You may not agree with me on this point; however, it is a fact that both of you will need this. It may also be a good idea for you and your spouse to discuss going for professional help from a certified marriage counselor.

Spend Some Time Alone

It is very important for you to spend time absorbing the truth bit by bit, thought by thought. This process is not for the faint of heart. You will need time, space and mental clarity to sift through the issues that you are now faced with. Hence, the fewer voices, opinions, beliefs, perspectives and ideas that you hear at this point is crucial. Having those few cornerstone confidantes is what you need during this time to make a well thought-out decision. Please, bear in mind that healing takes mental clarity, (to be clear about your desires) concerted effort and time. Hence, be deliberate and patient with yourself.

As you spend time sifting through the issues surrounding your relationship, do not spend time condemning or being too hard on yourself. Even if you have analyzed the situation and honestly realize that you have done some things wrong in your relationship, be kind, warm and forgiving to yourself. In this healing process, adopting the philosophy of 'self-love' is extremely important. Understanding the fact that we all have made mistakes in our relationships (I am sure your husband has made many) is a healthy mindset to adopt during this season. Embracing this philosophy of forgiveness is a crucial part of selflove and learning the secrets of healing infidelity in your marriage.

Can You Handle the Truth?
Moments of Truth (Be Completely Honest)

Question 1

Have you established an environment in your home where you and your spouse can have an honest conversation about infidelity?

■ Yes   ■ No

Question 2

Do you make it a habit of being an honest and reflective wife? (Just in case there are issues in the relationship that you need to address. Weaknesses as a wife that you may need to confront)

■ Yes   ■ No

Question 3

Would you emasculate, belittle and embarrass your husband if you found out that he committed infidelity? (Don't look at me like that ladies; you know exactly what I am talking about)

- Yes
- No

Question 4

If my husband committed infidelity and wanted to recommit himself to the marital relationship, would he feel comfortable to tell me the truth?

- Yes
- No

Question 5

If you found out that your husband cheated or is cheating on you, what steps would you take to healthily address the situation to facilitate the healing process? (Please include whether you would tell friends, neighbors, coworkers, children, boss, family members, get professional help and or seek guidance from a spiritual leader. Explain how you would engage the confrontation process)

Eight (8) Most Important Factors

These are the eight (8) most important factors that men said

triggered

and

sustained

their relationship with the other woman. Sixty-five (65%) percent of these men stated that if these issues were addressed, they would recommit themselves to the marital relationship.

We must spend time arming ourselves with this information so that we can activate the work needed to heal infidelity in our marriages.

Secret #1

Intentional Attention

As wives, we must understand that wishing, dreaming, having good intentions, great desires and an honest heart will not heal and create the marriage that we want. Those elements by themselves just do not cut it! We must be clear on the fact that the other woman makes it her diligent duty to 'love' and express that 'love' intentionally and deliberately to our men. She ensures that she lures and entraps them. It is clear to her that she must be intentional and deliberate with her goals for this man. She is focused and targeted in making sure that her execution style is on point.

Sometimes, some women may even do this genuinely, in that a woman will see a man that she likes, he immediately piques her interest; she then proceeds to make it her point of duty to show this interest. Not all women who commit infidelity with a married man at first intentionally goes out of her way to defile him and destroy a home. A woman might simply meet a man that sparks her interest and sets out to give him that intentional attention that she thinks he deserves. Even if she knows that he is married, she may be genuinely interested in him as an individual. Hence, she does not engage her interest to defile the sacredness of his marital vows. It may just be to show her genuine interest in him as a person. For example: checking in with him to find out how he is doing, inquiring about his day, inquiring to see whether or not he has eaten as yet, is he feeling better? And even possibly trying to encourage him to work on the relationship with his wife and so on, just giving him caring attention.

However, whether she sets out to intentionally defile this married man or care for him as an individual, once an interest is sparked, she makes sure that her smile, tone, language, and gestures are appealing enough to attract the object of her desire, 'that man'. She makes sure that he sees her smile, feels her warmth, and is smitten by her personality. Caring to be around, she creates a low-stress environment, paying attention to the little details about him.

Let's be real ladies, can you imagine how difficult this would be for a married man. A married man whose wife is not showing him this level of intentional attention or even half of this deliberate attention, especially if this attention is being supplied to him at a time when he is spiritually, mentally and emotionally depleted, when he feels very weak and vulnerable; this scenario presented to you is not a joke;

research for this book has shown that sixty-six percent (66%) of married men confessed to have committed infidelity. For some of these men, the decision to cheat was intricately tied to the other woman's deliberate and intentional attention.

In responding to the question of what attracted them and kept them going back to this other woman, some men explicitly stated that it was *"her warm and sensitive personality", "how she made me feel", "her high level of attention, appreciation and affection", "lack of attention from my wife and opportunity", "love, affection and attention" and "giving more attention to me."*

Hence, ladies the big question would be, what does a man mean when he says "her high level of attention, appreciation and affection", "giving me more attention" or "the way she made me feel". As you can imagine, every husband's interpretation of the word '*attention*' here would be different. Even though the word '*attention*' was used several times in response to the question, each man's meaning of the word would be different. Hence, we've come to the part of this book where we need to understand what does your man mean when he says I need more attention?

To answer this question, it is imperative that you and I spend some time understanding Gary Chapman's theory on *'The 5 Love Languages'*. Gary Chapman, the author of *'The 5 Love Languages'* spends a considerable amount of time explaining how men and women interpret and communicate love in a relationship. Hence, it's imperative that as wives, we understand the behavioral practices that will make our partners feel satisfied, fulfilled and happy. As wives, we must invest time, effort and energy to understand the principles found in this book, (*The 5 Love Languages*) so that we can become a bit more intentional and clearer about the type of attention to feed our men with. You will no longer spend time misfiring, or guessing what will make your spouse feel fulfilled and happy. You will now become more pointed, targeted and deadly like a bullet. A bullet that has been loaded with confidence and purpose, ready to execute in your marriage. Remember, the ultimate goal of every relationship should be to adequately satisfy the needs of our partners. Being armed with the right knowledge will make us into master executioners, armed and dangerous ready to execute in this dimension called 'love'.

Every human being on the face of this earth when speaking about 'feeling loved' and 'being loved' interprets and experiences that love differently. Hence, it is vital to know what actions to use to bring about true intimacy and connection with our partners. Knowing what 'actions' your partner will interpret as authentic, undiluted love, is a necessity in this love dimension.

So, spend some time to read this book, if you don't have the time to read the entire book, read the summary or listen to the audiobook.

A wise man by the name of Dr. Myles Munroe, in one of his marriage seminars said something that I will never forget. He said, 'A car needs gas to perform at its optimal level. On the other hand, as human beings, you and I need water to survive. If you fill your car tank with water, it will malfunction, and as human beings, if we drink gasoline, we will die.' (Munroe, n.d.)

Lesson: You can't give an individual what you feel/think they need. You must give that person that which you are 'sure' they need in order for them to operate at their highest level. And in return, they will provide you with what you need to become your best self.

Hence, the next biggest question would be, what is my husband's 'Love Language/s'? What can I do to make him feel valued, important and a top priority in our relationship? Don't sweat it ladies, to help us become effective couples, Gary Chapman has created a 'Love Language Test' that will help us to identify our partners 'Love Language/s'.

Hence, your first assignment from this book will be to go to google, review Chapman's theory on 'The 5 Love Languages' and complete the love language test together as a couple.

Tips on Getting Your Man to Complete This Test

I believe that if I am going to execute and bring excellence to this book, I must be completely transparent regarding the realities of married life. The truth is that sometimes, our spouses can be a bit difficult to deal with. In that, for some husbands, once you break out the paper and pen, a big wall of resistance may appear. For example, excuses like: I am tired, I can't be bothered, I don't have the time for that right now and I will get around to it (but never do). These are some excuses that some wives may face when trying to execute and become the best lover that they can be. However, if we are serious about living fulfilling lives as married couples, then we both need to execute on those tasks that will build our marriage.

Procrastination is the killer of all things, and if we are going to execute well, we must become tactful, harmless and subtle. Taking the bull by the horn. Hence, our approach must be non-threatening and alluring as wives. Here are a few ideas to help you with the task at hand:

- Secretly put the survey in his bag, attach an exotic gift with the following note affixed to it:

Baby, I want to lay it all out on the table for you tonight. But first I need to know what you like. Please, complete the survey and take it to the woman that will be laying it all out on top of the entire table for you tonight.

- Plan a special date night. While he's at work, send him an exotic text, after sending him this text, inform him that you have a special date night planned, but there is something important that you want him to do for you. Tell him what it is, bring the test on the date so that you guys can do it together. (make sure the place is conducive for this; make sure it is intimate, quiet, private and well lit)

Right now, I can see some ladies' facial expressions and twirling eye balls. However, I know exactly what I am talking about. My husband is not a pen and paper guy. He is not intrigued by these types of things, however, in understanding the benefit of honestly completing this test, I realized that I had to come up with a strategy to get this done. These suggestions may seem a bit excessive! however, remember, you are becoming a master craftsman and executioner in the art of love. Hence, your strategies and execution style must be as deadly and pointed as a skilled marksman.

Intentional Attention
Moments of Truth (Be Completely Honest)

Activity 1

Have you and your husband completed Gary Chapman's test on the 5 Love Languages? (You are encouraged to do this test so that you can become a pointed and targeted lover. If you or your spouse have not yet completed the test please make the effort to do so)

■ Yes ■ No

Activity 2

What is my husband's primary love language/s?

_____
_____
_____
_____

Activity 3

Use the knowledge of your husbands love language/s to create a simple plan for the next three (3) months. Identify simple things that you can do on a fairly consistent basis to give him that intentional attention that he deserves. (The key to having success is to make the actions/habits very simple so that you will be consistent.)

_____

_____

_____

_____

_____

_____

_____

_____

_____

Secret #2

Communication Secrets for Wives

Don't Force Your Man to Think Like You

Communication is a complicated process for a lot of couples because both individuals were cultured differently. Their thoughts, ideologies, principles and even value system, based on how they were raised and socialized can be very different. As you can imagine, when two different ideologies, principles and value systems come together to coexist under the same roof. The odds are that more than likely, there will be a battle 'a clash of the minds. In this 'clash of the minds', there is sometimes repeated verbal conflict/s between the two; a struggle to control and dominate each other's way of thinking. Although at times, we don't want to admit this. The truth is that we often want our partner to think like us. We would love it if they adopted most, if not all, of our ideals and principles.

Hence, this battle wreaks statements like: my way of thinking is right, and your way of thinking is wrong! I know that my way of thinking is more right than yours! This is where the biggest problem lies and so there is a constant struggle to make our partner accept and embrace our ideologies, value system, mental and moral compass. The truth is that if we are honest with ourselves, no one person has the complete knowledge about a thing, no one person has the complete truth and revelation about life itself. Hence, we see life and the world around us, predominantly from our vantage point, which encompasses our own limited personal experiences, our upbringing and social exposure.

However, this concept of 'truth' can be found outside of our own principles and ideologies. It then suggests that both individuals, more than likely have some degree /a measure of truth hidden within their thoughts. Hence, we both can approach the table of communication with valuable insights about various issues and the world in which we live. Ladies, when we force our spouse to think like us, this can be a very dangerous approach. In that as a human being, it is an unwelcome approach when we feel forced to do anything. As humans, we value our right to free will, which is a valuable part of our human experience. Even God in establishing a relationship with man gives us the right to have our own thoughts and ideologies in this expression of our free will.

Hey, don't get me wrong! I am not saying that it is wrong to attempt to influence or encourage your partner in taking a particular direction. The truth about it is, we are all susceptible to the power of influence, whether being influenced or to influence. As spouses, it is inevitable that we will influence each other. As we grow, the first recipient/s of that influence will be our spouses, friends and immediate family members. Ladies, I can't tell you the number of times my husband has reminded me of situations where I encouraged him to remain honest, as we struggled financially in our primitive years. He speaks about those days with such pride and joy about the times when I influenced him, held him to accountability and a standard of honesty.

However, there is a big difference between trying to influence versus attempting to control an individual. In influencing someone, we try to use our power of persuasion to lead them in the direction that we think is best. However, we still allow the power of choice to lie solely in their hand. On the other hand, the term control speaks to influencing an individual while trying to take away their right to choose. Ever so often, if we are honest with ourselves, we will admit that we have been guilty of trying to strongly force our principles, beliefs and philosophies on our spouses. If these ideologies are not received and accepted, then this can cause a problem in the relationship.

Ladies, your man does not like to be controlled. He doesn't like it when he is forced to think or adopt a particular way of thinking. Generally, men like to arrive at a conclusion on their own, after much deliberation within themselves. When a man arrives at his own decision using his own free will, when he is allowed to exercise the power of his own choice, then he is left with a feeling of autonomy and control. If you have been in a committed relationship for a while, then you know that a man thrives on control and autonomy. These two ingredients are vital components that will leave him *'feeling like a man'*, a man that is in control and in charge.

Connection and Agreement is Still Important

On the other hand, ladies, I want us to also know that connecting and bonding emotionally over critical issues is extremely important to your man. Women tend to think that men are not emotional beings, and that is somewhat true. However, your man relies a great deal on his feelings. In that, wherever a man feels connectivity, fusion and synchronization, that is where he will lay his head. When a man finds a woman that believes in his key ideas, thoughts and perspectives, this brings him a sense of importance and a feeling of being wanted. Listening and validating his way of thinking is crucial to him feeling like a man. You may not agree with all his ideas, and that's okay. But the worst thing that you can do is to make your man feel like his thoughts and opinions are not that valuable and important.

This was a key element explained to me by some men who completed my questionnaire. Some men, when probed, were clear to highlight the 'connection' that they felt with this other woman. One man in his explanation said it like this, *"she made me feel like a man"*, *"she made me feel as if my ideas and views were important and valuable"*. Some other men said the following: "the *other woman was easy to talk with*", *"she was easy to be around"*, *"she valued and supported my dreams, visions, perspectives, ideas and ideologies"*. As I read through these responses, it became obvious to me that these women had the ability to make these men feel at home and important in their spaces. These men felt a great connection between themselves and the other woman.

I know that as wives, this may be difficult for some of us to hear. However, this is the truth. It is so important that when interacting with our men, we approach them with this revelation in mind. As we intentionally interact with them daily, we must ensure that they feel connected and joined to us. One key ingredient in bringing about this connection is to allow them to feel our support with their visions and ideas. When their views, ideas, and visions land on fertile ground within our hearts, this will no doubt bring about agreement and connection within the relationship, which will ultimately heal our marriage, producing an invisible glue that will sustain us for years to come.

Finding Common Ground Is a Good Place to Start

When trying to build good communication with our spouses, finding common ground is an excellent place to start. Finding common thoughts, ideas and principles that both of you agree on, is crucial. Bear in mind, that if you are in a solid, mutually fulfilling relationship, then both of you must have some things in common. Something must have attracted you to each other. There is no attraction without some form of common ground. Two individuals cannot walk unless they agree (Amos 3:3, King James Version). When couples find and share common grounds, they create a sedimentary glue that can be used to solidify the entire structure of their relationship. When people find shared passions, interests, ideas, principles and convictions, these can become powerful tools in gluing the fragments of their relationship together. Find these shared passions, interests and ideas and build on them, through deliberate planning and intentional effort.

Spend Time Listening

Whatever your man spends time talking about daily are

indicators of the things he values dearly. The thoughts, ideas and principles that are important to him are sprinkled all over his conversations. The things that matter to him can be found in his constant communication with you. Oh, and by the way, we are not only speaking about what he is saying to you regularly but also his deliberate and noticeable acts of silence. Listen keenly! What is he constantly speaking about? You may not like this, but I am going to go there anyway. What are his constant critiques about you? What marital issues is he continually speaking to you about? What are the issues that he avoids deliberately speaking to you about? Be honest with yourself. Is there any degree of truth embedded within his constant ramblings? I am not saying that his critiques are entirely right or fair. I am only saying that deeply embedded within his complaints, incessant ramblings and conversations are found the issues that are more than likely important to him.

For years, my husband would constantly speak to me about making sure that the environment in which we lived had a certain level of structure, order, comfort and standard. He would constantly speak to me about this when things in our home were out of order. However, these issues were not as important to me. Please, understand that growing up in my formative years, I was known as a 'barrel child'. (A child whose parent/s left Jamaica to work in another country.) Hence, my mother was not around to spend time teaching me some of the pertinent ingredients needed for me to become an excellent homemaker. My upbringing and socialization somewhat lacked the guided hand of a mother. Yes, my eldest sister was there to groom me. However, not having the guided hand of a mother at that time still affected me.

On the other hand, my husband was cared for and nurtured by his grandmother. He was socialized, orientated and trained in being a man that could run a home efficiently from an early age. So, when we got married, I entered my marriage yes, with the understanding that I was to become the best homemaker that I could be. However, because these traits were not ingrained in me, I struggled greatly with this area of my life. But for my husband, structure was naturally a top priority for him. For me, structure had to become a learned discipline.

I would constantly hear his murmurings and see the displeasure on his face whenever he walked through the door, and our home was not in the condition that he wanted it to be. However, it was as if I heard, I saw but didn't understand the magnitude and importance of this issue to him. It took me a while to finally understand how truly important this issue was for his peace of mind and happiness. It really took me a while to understand that this issue was not just important to him, it was a crucial necessity for his mental stability and fortitude. A need that appealed to the deep psychological core of his being.

I believe that, it is safe to say that being married for over fifteen (15) years has given me some level of wisdom in helping couples. I am not suggesting that I have in any way arrived at perfection, heavens no! But based on my years of experience, I have learned this simple fact. If you listen keenly to your husband's chatter, then the things that are important to him will manifest themselves.

Become Fully Human

Someone once said to me, "This is Life and Life Happens to Everyone". As I read through the feedback provided by these fifty (50) men, I felt honored because I realized that some of these men were sharing with me the most intimate moments of their lives. Some of these men have never spoken so intimately regarding this issue that unfolded in their lives. Perusing through one questionnaire, I came across a man who left an indelible mark on my heart. This man, wherever he lives in the world, was experiencing a long-distance relationship with his wife. Hence, to fill that gap, he decided to have an extramarital affair.

As I read through the questionnaire, one of his responses to a question left me stunned and reflective. The question was: would you fully recommit yourself to the marital relationship if things changed? (paraphrasing) He responded by saying: "Yes", I then asked him why? and his response was, "because I love my wife". This was not the response I was looking for. I am not sure what response I was looking for. But this was not it. This man's response broke my heart and left a mark inside my soul.

I can imagine that some wives at this point would call me stupid and naïve. However, I am an authentic individual who becomes fully human when interacting with people. The truth of the matter is that this man is in a challenging situation. I don't have to agree with his actions to be human and understand his plight. I may not agree with his infidelities, but that does not stop me from being fully human, understanding that when this man's need call out to him, his wife is not there to satisfy them. I remember one day, my husband entered our bedroom and started to indicate to me that he wanted to have sex. At the time, I was experiencing intermittent back pains. Hence, I was a bit hesitant in supplying his needs. He spent about two (2) minutes massaging my back and then said to me: "Deciann I want some sex", he then said, "yes my brain understands that you are in pain and you are hurting, but my body wants to have sex". In my head, I began laughing because I knew exactly what he meant. This man knows that having an extra-marital affair is wrong. He fully understands that he is guilty as charged and should be sentenced. However, ever so often, when the need to be satisfied arises, he is faced with a serious dilemma. His wife is thousands of miles away and is unable to satisfy his needs. Ladies let me repeat. I don't have to agree with him to understand his plight. I can completely disagree with his actions while still being human enough to understand the complexity of the situation that he is in.

This truth is that long-distance relationships are not for the faint of heart. If you have never been away from your partner for a lengthy period of time, then you have no clue about the challenges associated with this lifestyle. If you have never experienced a significant rise in your libido, if you have never seriously felt the overwhelming urge to have sex, then ladies, you have no clue as to the struggle and challenge that takes place in situations like these.

I kid you not, as I became an older, more mature woman entering my mid to late thirties (30s). I began to experience a surge, a mighty rushing surge in my sexual appetite. Mighty God of Daniel! I thought I was going to die! No seriously. My libido significantly increased to the point where I felt as if I would have a psychosis. I would be at work and can't focus (anybody knows what I am talking about?). I couldn't wait to reach home and unleash myself on my husband. And by the way on one of these occasions, my husband was away visiting his family. For the first time, I knew what it felt like to have physical pain in my body because I wanted to have sex. Nearer my God to thee! One night, I had to run to the doctor to ask him if he could give me a medical intervention that would lower my sex drive. (I may be laughing now ladies, but at the time, it was far from funny.)

Now, before I go any further, let me take a brief moment here to have a repentance session. Steve, where ever you are right now, I repent! No, I diligently repent for all the times that you were burning up to have sex with me and I said "no Steve not tonight", "I am so tired" or "I can't be bothered". I repent now with the Holy Ghost and fire in front of all these witnesses both in heaven and on earth! Ladies, if you have never felt this surge, you are in for a drastic awakening. It was this experience that allowed me to understand the crisis that someone enters into when their sexual partner is not easily accessible.

Being able to be human and empathetic is a vital ingredient in forming a strong bond and connection with your man. You must create an environment where your man feels free to speak with you in the most challenging and vulnerable times of his life. In these instances you should be able to listen to him and understand his plight in a non-judgmental way, whilst offering sound advice. When interacting with your husband, allow him to become vulnerable and fully human with you. Being fully human does not mean that you will agree with his stance or decisions, but it does mean making him feel as if you can identify with his plight or struggle.

Learn How to Balance Your Emotional and Rational Self

As women, there are some inherent traits that are unique and natural for us. These traits serve us well in successfully navigating the world around us. These unique attributes are key in us becoming successful caregivers, mothers, lovers, C.E. O's of great companies and boss women in our various fields. However, if these natural traits are not managed carefully, then they can become a deterrent to our men and the people whom we serve. One of these inherent natural traits is the ability to connect with our emotions to engage the situations around us. Without controversy, this ability to form that emotional bridge is extremely crucial in us becoming great lovers, caregivers and human beings. However, if we do not learn how to manage and balance our emotions, then this priceless gem can at times become an undesirable trait.

Ladies, this single piece of advice is necessary for effectively communicating with our men in creating a seamlessly easy, effortless and low stressed environment. We must learn to become less emotive at times, and more rational, creating a perfect synergy between the two. I can almost hear the mental chatter in some wives' heads right now, as they rebut, argue and question some of the ideas highlighted in this book as they scream, What! What the hell! Really! However, ladies, it's true, being a woman for almost forty (40) years (I am laughing right now). I have seen and heard about the emotional persona's of women who push away their husbands, complicate their everyday relationships and even create an unwanted synergy in the workplace. The fact is that women tend to be very emotional at times, and when this emotional drive is not managed properly, it can create great stress and havoc.

For those women who have great rebuttals regarding this advice, I will be the first to say, I can understand your reaction. However, I can also relate to this simple truth that I have learned as a wife. The day I became less emotional, more logical and rational thinking, was the day my marriage got a little better. Conversations got a little easier. We could speak about very intense topics, and I could control my emotions. Remaining calm allowed me to get through conversations a bit more gracefully (even on issues regarding infidelity). Oh, don't be deceived, yes, I still do throw my emotional fits, but I have learned that if I remain calm and less emotional, then more than likely, the outcome will be better. Conversations became a little easier, and the stress thermometer in our relationship became lower. I am able to think clearer, and the communication process between my husband and I, have become a little smoother.

Communication Secrets for Wives
Moments of Truth (Be Completely Honest)

Activity 1

Do you allow your husband to freely express his ideas and perspectives in a comfortable environment, even if they are different from yours?

- Yes
- No

Activity 2

Create a list of topics and interests that you and your spouse can use to foster greater connection.

_____

_____

_____

Activity 3

What issue/s does your spouse continuously complain about? (regarding your relationship)

_____
_____
_____
_____
_____
_____
_____
_____

Activity 4

Which issue listed above needs your most urgent attention?

_____
_____

Activity 5

Create a plan and say how you will work to improve this issue

Secret #3

When the Cat is Away or Doesn't Make Deliberate Time to Play, will the Mice Stay or be Tempted to Find Someone Else to Play With?

When I was first getting to know my husband, one thing that struck me the most, was his playfulness with me. When spending time alone with him, he would be all over me like a cat would be all over a furry ball of thread. He loved to play! This was the attribute that struck me the most about him because I was the opposite. I was much more composed and subdued, even in private moments with him. However, he was like a cat in its cot playing with a ball of thread [which was me]. This was one of the things that struck me the most about the man that I was presently dating. Honestly, this extremely playful side of my then boyfriend terrified me a little. Because I wondered how long was, I going to be able to keep up with this insatiable appetite to play. Needless to say, he got much more mature and subdued. However, that playful side is still embedded in him, and once I use all the right keys at the right time, these attributes can be activated at a moment's notice. The truth is that I have thought about this inherent need that my husband has to play. Through playing, he bonded with me to feel that connection and intimacy that he craved as a man. Hence, let me ask a crucial question. What if I should leave our nest for an extended period of time? What if I should leave him in Jamaica and go to work in a foreign country for a while? Don't get me wrong! I am not asking these questions to offend, condemn or criticize anyone. I am just endeavoring to have an honest and open conversation with us as women. Let me rephrase these questions again, what if I [the snuggly fur ball] should leave our nest for an extended period? What do you think would happen with my playful husband? Who would my husband play with? How would he feel when this need for connection and intimacy arise, and I am not there? If I am not there, will he find someone else to fill this need? What if I don't make the deliberate time for him to play with me? Finally, this is the big question: When the Mice is away, is there any possibility that the cat will be tempted to find someone else to play with? Let's be honest and real for a moment, as we attempt to engage in this discussion regarding the importance of proximity and spending meaningful time with our spouse.

In having this discussion, a few of the husbands who took part in my research come to mind. As mentioned before, one of these husbands' situation appealed to me and caused me to begin thinking. And I would like us to closely examine his situation a little more, by examining his responses to the questions asked.

Excerpt from the questionnaire

- What is your current relationship status?

Response: Married

- While being married, have you ever had a sexual relationship with any female other than your wife?

Response: Yes

- In your opinion, what triggered this temptation to commit infidelity?

Response: Distance

- What most attracted you to this other woman?

Response: She is closer in distance hence; she had more to offer me

- If your wife began to exhibit most or even some of the core qualities that you found in this other female, would you recommit yourself to the marital relationship?

Response: Yes

- If yes, why? Explain

Response: Because I love my wife

The day I read this questionnaire, something inside of me was deeply touched as a woman and as a wife. Some women would have read this questionnaire and respond by saying really, liar! However, I am wondering if as wives we are so immortal that we are unable to be human and realistic for a moment. To have the ability to disagree with this man's actions but also exhibit that level of human understanding, which is required when dealing with real-life situations that at times confront us. This man's wife has seemingly left their nest for an extended period of time. When he rolls over in the nights to play with his furry ball, there is a space where she once occupied. When he's in the mood to connect and bond with his cat, she's gone. When he comes home from a hard day at work and needs a mental, emotional, psychological and sexual release, his cat is no longer there.

Now in all honesty, can't you see the dilemma that this man is in, yes, he still loves his wife. However, as a man, he is wired to connect, bond and mate with his woman. So, can you imagine the challenging situation that unfolds itself, in his moment of loneliness? As I have repeated many times, I am not a supporter of infidelity. Infidelity is wrong, and that's the truth.

However, as we engage the challenges of life, we must become realistic individuals. I may not agree with his choice of committing infidelity. However, that does not mean that I can't understand and empathize as a human being with his need for connection and bonding.

Can we spend a moment ladies, to just have an authentic heart to heart discussion? Setting aside deliberate time for bonding as a couple is crucial. Allocating regular time for intimacy [not only sex but talking, laughing and sharing] with your man is a must if we intend to maintain a healthy relationship with our men. I remember years ago when I was studying. I was consumed with school and the various demands that were being made of me. One day while talking with my husband, he revealed to me that he was lonely.

He understood that I was studying to provide a better quality of life for us as a family. However, despite understanding this reality, this did not stop him from experiencing boredom and loneliness in our marriage. To me, everything was reasonably fine. I was so focused on achieving an excellent tertiary level education that I didn't realize what was happening.

However, to him he was facing a great mountain in our relationship. It was not until I realized what was taking place in his heart, that I started to understand a little more about the challenge that he was having, as a man. One day, he said to me, "Deciann, a man is like a glass, he can hold a certain amount. When you fill me up and send me into the world, I feel complete as if I can face the world victoriously. On the other hand, when you don't fill me, I feel weak, unsure of myself and defeated." If as wives, we neglect to understand this genuine need that our lovers have, then we are setting ourselves up for more battles in our marriages.

Another man who participated in my research wrote the following:

Excerpt from the questionnaire

- What is your current relationship status?

    Response: Married

- While being married, have you ever had a sexual relationship with any female other than your wife?

    Response: Yes

- What most attracted you to this other female companion?

    Response: Her Time for Me

- Please describe the primary feeling/s that you experienced while being with the other female companion?

   Response: Always Listen

- When you were with this other woman, what top three (3) activities did you engage in to sustain these feelings?

   Response: Good Communication, Time Management and Feeling Happy

- What kept you going back to this other woman?

   Response: Her Time

- What attribute/s did you love about this other woman that you wish your wife had?

Response: Attention, Time Management and Make Me Feel Important

- What kept you going back to this other woman?

   Response: Her time

- In your opinion, what do you believe honestly lead to you having a sexual relationship with the other woman?

   Response: Time

- If your wife began to exhibit most or even some of the core qualities that you found in this other female, would you recommit yourself to the marital relationship?

Response: Yes

- If yes, why? Explain?

Response: Because I Would Not Be Lacking in Any Area

Again, ladies, we may be very critical and judgmental about this man's actions. However, if we analyze his words, we would observe that he repeats the word *'time'* six times (6x). Isn't it clear that this man craves nesting and spending time with his wife, to feel fulfilled and connected? Isn't it clear that if this couple deliberately creates the time to muse and bond with each other, then this decision would significantly improve the quality of their relationship? Wouldn't this be a step in the right direction to heal infidelity in their marriage?

Undoubtedly one of the most unexpected revelations that I

received when investigating about infidelity and the other woman, is the fact that this relationship often supplied a lack, want or need that these men had. For me, it was the way some of these men humanized these women. It was not only about sex. It was also about the companionship that these relationships provided. Some of these women spent time talking, laughing, having deep riveting conversations, playing, cooking and going out with these men. Obviously, some of these relationships were fed with deliberate acts of bonding and spending time together. The other women made sure to maximize the time that they had together. They wasted no time! They carved out the time needed to sustain their relationship for as long as they wanted. So, I ask this question again, *when the cat is away or doesn't make deliberate time to play, will the mice stay or be tempted to find someone else with whom to play?*

When the Cat is Away or Doesn't Make Deliberate Time to Play, Will the Mice Stay or Be Tempted to Find Someone Else to Play With?
Moments of Truth
(Be Completely Honest)

Activity 1

As a couple, do you have scheduled date nights?

- Yes
- No

Activity 2

If yes, how often do you go on dates?

- Often
- Sometimes
- Seldom
- Never

Activity 3

Use both your love languages to create a list of meaningful activities that you would both enjoy doing as a couple?

(visit the official website for The Dating Divas and get some great dating ideas)

Activity 4

Carve out some meaningful time together by creating a dating plan. (Include: place/event that you are thinking of going together, budget, day, time, babysitting arrangements and so on.)

_____
_____
_____
_____
_____
_____
_____
_____
_____
_____
_____

Secret #4

Sexual Terrorist in the Bedroom

> - What characteristic/s did you love most about this other woman that you wish your wife had?
>
> **Response: Being a sexual terrorist in the bedroom.**
>
> - In your opinion, what do you honestly believe lead to you having a sexual relationship with this other woman?
>
> **Response: I felt there was no sexual connection with my wife.**

This was an actual response from one respondent who completed my questionnaire. I decided to begin this chapter with this particular response because this phrase seems to generally reflect the desire of the men who spoke about sex, their wives and the other woman. Ladies, as I attempt to reflect and mirror the hearts, desires and minds of our men as it relates to sex, it is imperative that we have an honest discussion about this issue.

Let me first say that some of the men who completed these questionnaires did not leave any ambiguity regarding the sexual pleasure that they received from the other woman. Wives, I know that this can be an uncomfortable and unwelcome discussion for some of us. However, let me make it unequivocally clear that the intent of this author is not to issue any blame to wives. However, I will say this again and again, if we are serious about healing infidelity in our marriages, then we must be assertive and aggressive towards fixing the issues concerning our relationships.

If you think that sex is a little important to your man, if you think that sex is somewhat important to your man, if you think that sex is important or very important to your man, ladies, these statements may not fully reflect your husband and his need for sex.

Sex for your husband is a regular necessity just like 'water to a thirsty man', 'air to the breathless' and 'food to the hungry'. You may be tempted to take these statements lightly, or even make fun of my analogies. However, these views regarding 'sex' came straight from the 'horse's mouth' from the men who admitted to me that they committed infidelity. These fifty (50) men entered into the confession hall of my survey, and most of them did not hide their true feelings about the sexual pleasure that they received from the 'other woman'. Some of these men explicitly shared with me sexual encounters that I am sure that they have not shared with anyone. Hence, I believe that we should give our greatest attention to the ideas and principles found in this chapter.

Here are a few of the questions and actual responses from some of these men who participated in the survey:

Excerpt from questionnaire

- In your opinion, explain what triggered the temptation to commit infidelity?

"Lack of sex"

"Poor sex"

"My wife was boring in bed; she goes to sleep in clothes."

"Well, a lack of sex"

- What characteristic/s did you love most about the other woman, that you wish your wife had?

"I wish my wife was a sex beast."

"I wish my wife was a good sexual woman and love maker."

"Her sex drive"

- In your opinion, what do you believe honestly lead to you having a sexual relationship with the other woman?

"Because my wife did not love sex"

"Wanting good sex"

"My wife didn't love sex."

- What kept you going back to the other woman?

"The Good Sex"

"She was good in bed."

"To have good sex with her"

"Her passion for sex"

- What most attracted you to the other woman?

"She can sex very bad."

"Her way she does sex is magnificent. She is a sex maniac."

Ladies, these are just some of the responses that reflect our men regarding sex. Let me also add that there were a few responses about sex and the other woman, which were too explicit for this forum. Hence, the issue is real ladies and in need of our attention as wives. So, let's be fearless and start this discussion

First Thing, Leave the Wife Material at the Bedroom Door

In responding to one of my questions, one man summed it up quite well. He said, "Often, our sexual preferences are hard to find in what we presume as wife material." This man further explained that it is difficult to find a woman that has the bedroom proclivities, shape and moral standards that specifically appeals to you as a man. He highlighted the fact that if synergy is not achieved in these three areas, then this can cause a problem in the relationship.

Frankly speaking, a wife is normally a particular type of woman. One that has great moral standards and qualities that a man normally looks for when he is thinking about settling down. In searching for a wife, men often go in search of a woman who has the qualities that he can take home and introduce to his mother. He looks for the individual who he believes will be instrumental in taking care of his home and children. The person who he can introduce to his boss, cooperate partners and proudly show off to the world. However, the truth about the matter is that, sometimes it is difficult to find a woman with the complete package. One that sparks his interest, has a high moral standard, very responsible, caring, kind, a nurturer by nature and sexually compatible with him as a man.

Now, let's compare the responses presented by some husbands regarding their 'wives' and 'the other woman'.

Wives

"My wife was boring in bed."

"My wife is boring in bed; she goes to sleep in clothes."

"Lack of sexual activity between my spouse and me also boring sex."

"Not getting enough sex. My wife was always tired."

"My wife just can't sex good."

The Other Woman

"The Good Sex"

"She can sex very 'bad'."

"Her way she does sex is magnificent. She is a sex maniac."

"Her passion for sex."

Ladies, I am sure that at this point, some of us have great objections, rebuttals and have taken great offense to the statements made by these men. However, to solidify and fortify our marriages, it behoves us to think less with our emotional minds and more with our logical/rational minds. Let me say again if we are serious about this investment that we have made in our lives, then we know that getting angry, throwing a temper tantrum and cursing our husbands will do little to help (although some of them deserve this, and it would feel good at the moment). We must now use our logical minds to become master strategists and executioners in this fight to save the investment that we have tirelessly worked hard to acquire.

We can sit around, curse the other woman, curse our husbands, complain about his mistakes and his faults (which some may be true) and list all his faults or flaws, but will these solve our problems? Will this approach give you the results that you are desperately yearning for in your marriage? Will using this approach make your marriage better? If it will, go straight ahead and utilize it! However, I can assure you that this approach will not draw your husband any closer to you. It will not bring the authentic change that you are yearning and seeking for within your marriage.

It's okay to be angry and perturbed regarding the unveiling of this information. However, if we want to achieve any measure of success in our relationship, then we must learn how to control and channel these feelings productively. For me, this research provides a sacred opportunity to learn and use this piece of information to create strategies that will solidify my marriage. We have now been given an unusual opportunity to get the uncensored version that goes on inside of a man's heart. ***So, ladies let's be fearless and get down to business.***

These men are clearly saying that even though they have chosen a woman with the quality and standards that can represent them in the world, when it comes to the bedroom, leave all that at the door! No matter how innocent your man looks, no matter how nonchalant he behaves when it comes to sex, don't use that behavior as a sign, as to how you treat your sex life. Don't be deceived!

Listen to me, wives, when making love to your man in and out of the bedroom, don't back down, don't be discreet or shy. 'Lay it on thick'... Bring you're A+ game to your sexual encounters with him. Let your husband cry like a baby. Let him get lost, in the pleasure that he is receiving from you. This is what God wants from you, not the other way around. God mandated you with this assignment. The day you said *'I do'* to this man, you made a vow to give your marriage you're A+ game. Do not under any circumstances relinquish this duty to anyone else; *you are his wife!*

When it comes to your man, the one to whom you said 'I do', you need not to be shy, shamefaced, timid, casual or discreet. You need to be assertive and direct with him in the bedroom. ***No Christian persona here!*** You need to give your man the wicked and wild sex. Ladies, let's be clear on this point, there are times when your man will enjoy you being assertive, a bit aggressive and direct, taking full control of your sexual extravaganza together.

Honestly, I can understand that the demands that are being made of us are a bit excessive and in the realm of superwoman, right? I know that as these requests are made, they may leave us feeling a bit overwhelmed and maybe angry because the truth is, in most of these extra-marital affairs, the demands and expectations are ridiculously uneven (of course, because it's an extra-marital affair). The playing field is not leveled, in that, as wives, the expectations, workload and demands are much more.

In most cases, we are expected to assist in financially providing for our families. We are expected to be excellent homemakers, nurturers, great mothers, outstanding boss women in our various fields, exceptional lovers and so much more. Oh, and by the way, we are expected to achieve complete mastery or near mastery in all these areas. So ladies, I kid you not! I know that this job of being a wife is a ridiculously hard one. And I know that these demands are not for the weak or the faint of heart. Hats off to all the hardworking and dedicated wives who are right now reading this book!

Ladies, let me remind us of this simple fact, and it is the fact that 'the human brain' is a magnificent organ. The human brain can learn, relearn and adapt to anything it wants to. Anything we want or need to learn; we can learn it! There is no skill necessary for us to become the best in our fields that we cannot acquire! Hence, the challenge that we sometimes face in this area, (being a sexual terrorist in the bedroom) is the limitations that we place in our minds.

These limitations may include but are not limited to the following: *'I am not that kind of person', 'that's not naturally me', 'that is not my personality', 'I am not like that', 'really! I don't believe in this foolishness', 'I am too tired to have sex and he should understand' and 'I am trying my best and he should know that'*. Some of these thought patterns may be the uncensored discussion that's taking place in our minds as we read this book. And please note that these thought patterns just may be among the real reasons, why sometimes we are not able to rise to the occasion and execute as deliberately and fearlessly as we should.

In conducting the research for this book, fifty (50) wives were also asked to enter into the confession hall of my survey. Results from that survey reveal that eighty-one percent (81%) of wives admit that their husbands are the ones who most time initiate their sexual encounters. Now ladies this means that in eighty-one percent (81%) of marriages, the wives are more passive and the husbands are more aggressive, in activating their sexual encounters. Please take a moment to really think about that. Now do you think *'the other woman'* is passive and laid-back in this area? Heavens no! She is much more aggressive, forceful and direct. And this definitely helps to fuel the kind of sexual experience that takes place.

If we are going to become master strategists and executioners in our marriages, then we must begin to assert ourselves a little more in the bedroom. Now ladies, I hope that you do not think that you can enter into this arena with the arsenal that you have in your hand. To become proficient and the best in any field, you need to immerse yourself in attaining and mastering *'the knowledge'* required to execute at the highest level.

Hence, as wives it is crucial that we understand the following:

- Understand our individual bodies as women

- Know how to use the knowledge about our bodies to become better lovers

- Learn to master the skills needed in giving our husbands 'the good sex'

Therefore, as we begin this journey of becoming great sexual lovers, we must first be honest and ask ourselves some hard questions. There is no real growth without honesty!

Question 1.

Do you enjoy having sex?
- Yes
- No
- Sometimes

Question 2.

Are you as free as you want to be when having sex with your spouse or are you struggling to maximize the moment and enjoy your time together?

- Most times
- Sometimes
- Rarely
- Never

It's very important for you to pinpoint exactly what's fully hindering you from completely letting go and enjoying your sexual encounters with your husband. Below are some barriers that may be hindering your ability to perform sexually at your optimal level. Please spend some time thinking about these and doing your own little research about them.

Barriers to Good Sex…….

Good, better & best. Spend time trying to identify the core reason/s that's hindering you from performing at your best in the bedroom. According to Mayo Clinic (2019) these barriers to sex may include:

- Fatigue
- Illness
- Poor Body Image
- Past Sexual Trauma
- Low Sex Drive
- Low Self Esteem
- Depression
- Unresolved Issues in the Marriage
- Lack of Connection with Your Partner
- _____
- _____
- _____
- _____

Write your own barrier/s if you don't see it listed above.

Some Possible Solutions That Could Improve Your Sex Life

Price (2018) states that the following foods may improve your libido levels. These are:

- Ginseng
- Maca Root
- Dark Chocolate
- Libido Enhancer Supplements (e.g. Maca, Ginseng, Gingko Biloba and so on)
- Water
- Essential Oils
- Collagen –Rich Food
- _____
- _____
- _____
- _____
- _____
- _____

Do you own little research and make your own list.

Try a few and see what works best for you.

Ovulation, My Body and My Personal Experience.

I struggled with having a low sex drive for years in my marriage. My husband and I, would at times sit and speak about this issue. However, when I entered my mid to late thirties, I decided to stop taking my birth control. I am not sure why, however, I believe, it was the invisible hand of God in my marriage. As previously mentioned, I experienced an unusual spike in my libido levels. My sex drive increased by about two hundred percent (200%). I kid you not! On the onset of this spike, I even found it hard to concentrate on my work. I thought I was going to tear out my hair, run up and down the corridors, (I work in a school) lose my mind and die!

However, one of the most crucial revelations that I got as a wife from these crazy experiences was the fact that if I listened to my body and knew my ovulation days, sex during these times was soooo goooood. It was very erotic, intense and enjoyable for both of us. This, ladies is a part of my secret weapon. If I want to give my husband an enjoyable and intense sexual experience, if I want us to have great erotic sex, it is so much easier when I am ovulating; when my libido levels are much higher. Hence, if you are like me, then planning your date nights during this time of the month is best. When your libido levels are at its highest, you will be ready, armed and sexually dangerous to take your husband on an erotic journey.

Finally, ladies, we need to have this discussion of 'I love having sex with you but ....!'

An excellent place to start when deciding to execute in the bedroom is to know exactly what your husband likes. Does your husband have any fantasies? (By the way, all men do). What would he like to have on his plate and how would he like to have it? Ladies, this is an excellent time to have this honest and open conversation with your spouse. As his wife, it is your job to be fully aware of his sexual thoughts. Remember, reciprocity is essential in a marriage, for both persons to feel satisfied, fulfilled and happy.

And since we're being fearless as wives, let's go ahead and take this discussion a little further.

As we speak about having a sexually satisfying life with our spouses, it is important that we also have this discussion regarding sexual ethical rules in the bedroom (if we have any). Clearly, remembering one of the most disturbing but honest feedback from one of the men who completed my questionnaire. This man was engaged in what seemed like several extra-marital affairs. When he was probed about the possibility of recommitting to the marital relationship, he explicitly stated, 'no'. According to this man, he would never recommit to the marital relationship because his wife would not be willing to fulfill his sexual fantasy (extremely disturbing). This situation reveals to us the importance of knowing the mind and heart of our men regarding sex. Failure to understand this may cost us not only our happiness but also our literal lives.

Now let's be honest with our spouses and encourage them to be very transparent with us, regarding this quest for sexual pleasure. Be reminded that you cannot ask for the truth, unless you are prepared for the answers.

Bedroom ideas……………..

As we grow and expand ourselves, we must begin to build our bedroom arsenal by spending time planning and executing our plans. Here are a few interesting websites that will give you some great ideas in building your lethal weapon of love. I must say that I love 'The Dating Divas', they are never short of some good ideas. However, the challenge will be, spending enough time to find the strategies that best fit you as a couple.

A Few Website Suggestions:

■ The Dating Divas (sign up for their '7 Day of Love Program' it's free)

■ 16 Amazing Sex Tricks He May Want You to Know
https://www.redbookmag.com/lovesex/sex/advice/a111/amazing-sex-tricks/

- Top Fifty Kinky Ideas for Sexual Relationship
https://www.lovepanky.com/sensual-tease/passion

Sexual Terrorist in the Bedroom
Moments of Truth (Be Completely Honest)

Activity 1

Identify the main reason/s that's hindering you from experiencing complete pleasure and ecstasy with your spouse.

_____

_____

_____

Activity 2

What steps will you take to address these issues?

_____

_____

_____

_____

Activity 3

Have fun creating a night or evening of sexual rendezvous for you and your husband. Write out the details of your plans, which may include: your partners' sexual like/s, place, music needed to set the ambiance, sexual positions and items needed for magnificent love making. Remember, only focus on what will take place in the 'bedroom' NOT the
entire date).

_____

_____

_____

_____

_____

_____

_____

_____

Secret #5

Happiness Makes the Heart Grow Fonder

Happiness is definitely the desired goal of most if not, every couple who gets married. The need for every relationship to produce pure joy is crucial to its sustenance. This desire in creating an oasis, a literal safari within the relationship, is a necessity that no couple can deny. Hence, learning to facilitate authentic humor and laughter in a relationship is undeniably important.

Jeffrey Hall from the University of Kansas in his research spent time investigating thirty-nine (39) studies that sought to explain the importance of laughter in a relationship. In conducting his research, Hall stated that "playfulness between romantic partners is a crucial component in bonding and establishing relational security" (HuffPost, 2017). In other words, playfulness is that invisible glue that will foster greater intimacy and stability in your relationship.

According to Hall a key aspect in fostering authentic laughter and joy in your relationship is having the same sense of humor; identifying common things that both of you find humorous. Being able to chill, relax and have light moments of authentic laughter together is very important to the health of your relationship. Creating those moments of pure humor and relaxation is a must, if we want our marriage to produce the joy and intimacy, needed for it to last through the ages.

So, I guess my next big question would then be, when was the last time you and your life's partner had a good authentic laugh? When was the last time both of you spent significant time just relaxing, bonding and building intimacy through humor, laugher and play? Or has it just been all work and no play? Has it been mostly about work and little or no time to play? Let's just check ourselves ladies. Let's really pause for a moment and become naked and not ashamed in the sacredness of our own hearts.

The greatest adjustment for some married couples, is the reality that sinks in after the well-planned and anticipated wedding ceremony. After the honeymoon phase of dating, where butterflies filled the stomach, the feeling of blood rushing through the entire body, and the almost effortless gel that glued the relationship together. After this phase, there is a need to settle down and start a real life together. The demand for both individuals to provide for the family (in some cases), the pressure to care for the home, and eventually, the need to care for the little feet produced by the couple now becomes a new priority. One husband who completed my questionnaire coined it well when asked about infidelity in his marriage. He said that (fidelity) was the plan until the children came along and the dynamics of the marriage changed.

Wives let's be real here. Again, my ultimate dream for writing this book is not to condemn or point fingers at anyone. My ultimate goal, as the author, is for us to take another look at the man in the mirror, take the necessary steps in adjusting ourselves as we face the truth about our lives.

Isn't this man's situation the reality in so many marriages across the world? For some spouses, "fidelity" was the plan until the marriage became like a job. Their spouses like their coworkers and their home like their place of employment where the biggest goal is to cohabitate without having sustainable and meaningful interactions as husbands and wives.

These analogies may be a bit harsh. However, the truth is that somewhere along the line, some of us got caught up in living by our titles as 'wives', 'husbands', 'mothers' and 'fathers', we allowed these titles to define us, forgetting the fact that we should be lovers and life partners to each other. Lovers and life' partners on this journey of life, where the seasons are forever changing and the challenges sometimes become extremely treacherous. Forgetting the fact that we should be building bridges over troubled waters. Bridges that we will need to walk on in the next thirty (30), forty (40) and even fifty (50) years of our lives together as couples.

Undeniably, there is a need for us as couples to create that space for fun, joy, play and humor. Let's not be deceived ladies; without these vital ingredients, our marriages will become just like any other relationship. Where we often look and act the part; however, on the inside, we are only acquaintances occupying the same space together.

Happiness does make the heart grow fonder! Multiple researches conducted have echoed this fact - that laughter, play and humor are essential ingredients needed to keep any relationship.

After spending time reading through the responses received from my male participants, it is clear that some of these extra – marital affairs were sustained by these crucial components. To the extent, that twenty-three percent (23%) of these affairs ultimately became permanent relationships.

Happiness Makes the Heart Grow Fonder?
Moments of Truth
(Be Completely Honest)

Activity 1

Do you and your spouse usually use play, laughter and humor as bonding tools?

    Yes
    No

Activity 2

If 'no' why do you think this is?

_____

_____

_____

_____

_____

_____

_____

Activity 3

Research has shown that using humor as a bonding tool is more effective, when couples find the same things humorous. What life topics do you and your spouse find funny?

_____

_____

_____

_____

_____

_____

Activity 4

Intentionally carve out some time to just chill, relax and talk about these humorous topics.

Secret # 6

Remember! Your Man Eats with His Eyes First

Have you ever gone to dine at a restaurant, and as you sat there your tongue began to salivate and your stomach began to growl in waiting expectation, however, when the food arrived at your table, the presentation was so poor that you were immediately turned off? All of a sudden even though you were waiting in dear expectation, the presentation of that meal and how it was served to you immediately deactivate your desire to eat it. Let me ask you a honest question. Were you really hungry? Did you really want something to eat? The fact is that, you were sincerely waiting with great anticipation to eat your meal. But the appearance of the food and its presentation immediately sent a message to your brain which said, " no ", I don't want this to eat. Ladies think about that, just the presentation of anything, has the power to evoke or deactivate a psychological and physiological response to a thing.

It is often said that the first impression lasts. The truth is, what we see has a lot to do with our impression of anything. The sense of seeing is one of the senses that we greatly rely on, in engaging the world around us. Ladies, this basic principle is absolutely crucial in stimulating and maintaining your husband's interest in you.

It is a fact that men are attracted to a woman's physical appearance. Even some of the men who completed my questionnaires spoke about their physical attraction to the other woman. It was the woman's figure, shape, looks and general physical appearance that attracted and sustained their attraction to her. Ironically, even one of the men who stated that he had never committed infidelity, admitted that the temptation that he experienced was with the other woman's physical appearance. Now, ladies, can we deny the strong effect that the physical appearance of a woman has on a man?

We would be crazy to deny this! Hence, we must now use this knowledge to stimulate and sustain their attraction to us.

In the chapter on 'Sexual Terrorist in the Bedroom' I highlighted one of the participant's response regarding his wife and sex. Let me refresh our memory. He said: "My wife is boring in bed; she goes to sleep in clothes." Now ladies, just thinking about this man's response, undoubtedly reveals to us again, the reality that presentation matters! How your body is packaged, marketed and presented to your husband, matters!

Someone once told me that the definition of a 'mad person' is someone who keeps doing the same things repeatedly even though they know that it's not working. One of my most memorable stories in the Bible was the story of David and Saul. In this story, the Bible highlights the conflict that ensued between the two. Essentially Saul hated David and desperately wanted to kill him. The bible stated that in order for David to get the victory he had to operate under great wisdom and humility. To overcome this obstacle, David had to be wise as a serpent and harmless as a dove. (1 Samuel 19, New Life Version)

Ladies for us to achieve the level of success that we desire to see in our marriage, we too must apply ourselves to wisdom by being wise as a serpent and harmless as a dove. We must use this knowledge of our husbands' attraction to our physical appearance to stimulate and lure our husband's interest towards us. Again, don't get me wrong. I am not saying that our husbands will be faithful to us solely on the premise of physical attraction and appearance. I am simply saying that we cannot pretend or deny the importance of physical appearance and its impact on our men. We must understand that this is an inherent need that our men have. And we must make sure that we satisfy this need of making ourselves physically appealing to our spouses.

Remember! Your Man Eats with His Eyes First Moments of Truth
(Be Completely Honest)

Activity 1

Do you know the part/s of your body that your husband likes the most?

- Yes
- No

Activity 2

When was the last time you added something new to your clothing collection? Something that you know accentuates the part/s of your body that your husband likes?

- A month ago
- Three months ago

- Six months ago

- A year ago

Activity 3

Buy something new that will accentuate the part/s of your body that your husband likes.

Activity 4

Remember! Your man eats with his eyes first, so plan your attire for a week. Choose what you will wear for each situation within the week.

Work Wear-

House Wear-

Bedtime Wear-

Secret #7

His Blueprint Craves Your Support

Some time ago, a friend of mine shared with me her conversation with a recently separated married man, who at the time of this discussion was still hurting because of his recent separation from his wife. This man told the story that he had been married to his wife for over twenty years (20 yrs.) and that the marriage had produced two (2) children. He further explained that during these twenty (20) plus years, he became the primary breadwinner for his family. This man explained that he tried to empower his wife by sending her to school and by helping her to become an entrepreneur. However, according to him, both of these attempts failed. In that, his wife, after acquiring her accreditation, did not use her newfound skills in making herself marketable. He stated that, he assisted her in establishing a small business. However, because of her mismanagement, the business was not fruitful and had to be closed. Hence, he had to shoulder his family's financial burden alone. He single-handedly provided for his family, sent his children through school and secured a tertiary level education for them. Unfortunately, because of the adverse demand on his body, he eventually developed a lifestyle illness. This particular day in question, as he sought to mentally and emotionally unload himself, it was evident that the situation was still extremely painful for him. Hence, tears began to roll down his face as he recounted these events in his marriage. The fact is that he had been married to his wife for years, and so he saw value in his marital relationship. However, he believed that his wife was not willing to evolve and transition into that independent woman that he needed her to become.

All in all, he admits that his wife was a beautiful homemaker, in that, she made sure that the home and its surroundings were very appealing to him when he came home. However, the fact is that he needed additional support; he needed financial support from her. He needed his God-given helpmate to match his dollar with a half, or even a quarter of hers, but she did not.

Finally, he admits that he had met someone new. Someone who was an independent and industrious woman. A go-getter, an individual who was able to support his dreams, a woman that was willing and able to offer him financial assistance. The truth of the matter is that, although this man was still saddened by the loss of his marriage and how his separation unfolded, he was relieved that he now had a helpmate that was willing and able to assist him to lighten the financial burden. To match his dollar with half or even a quarter of hers.

In the book *'Act Like Lady, Think Like a Man'*, Steve Harvey spends a considerable amount of time helping ladies to understand the thought process and mindset of a man. The day I read this book; light bulbs went off in my head. Some things in my relationship now made sense. The effort, hard work, energy and passion that my husband exude in taking care of his family and pursuing his financial goals all began to make sense. The gray areas in my head as a wife, the questions I had as it relates to his priorities, now began to make sense.

As the man he is wired to take care of his family, by pursuing those activities that he believes will define him and bring the satisfaction that he seeks. That's his goal every morning and every night! Hence when it came to seeing him taking a more aggressive approach in the other areas of our marriage, he was not as aggressive. I used to complain and murmur about these changes that I wanted to see. However, reading this book has given me more clarity about the strategies that I needed to use, in order to become a more effective wife.

It was through understanding these principles that I began to understand the mind of my husband. And more importantly, the things that I could do to intricately place myself into his world. In receiving this mental shift, I realized that I needed to change my approach. When he has a business idea/s (and there are times when he has several), how could I fit myself in his plans and give him the support that he will need? Can I be honest with you? Sometimes, this is extremely difficult for me because I don't agree with some of his ideas. I can see all the advantages and disadvantages of his plans and sometimes, the disadvantages outweigh the advantages. However, understanding how crucial my support is to him. I must challenge myself to think of ways in which I can show my support to his ideas. I realize that if I do this with my whole heart, then there is a great possibility that our marriage would become stronger and better. And even if his business venture/s failed, I now understand that there is a learning curve in all of life's experiences. Challenging myself to realize that failure can strengthen us, if we allow it, I am aware that giving him my support is sometimes, all he needs to soar and become greater.

A Nigerian nurse once said to my husband, the role of a wife is to help her husband complete his thoughts. In other words, every man was born with his purpose and passion locked inside of him. He was born with a blueprint locked inside of his heart and mind. And the job of his spouse is to help him make sense of that blueprint and to assist him in bringing those plans to fruition.

Ladies need I say more to us? Your husband needs your support more than he is letting on. One participant in my research again said it like this: "I wish my wife would help me to bring out my dreams and visions to reality." Often our men seem to be so tough, as if they could conquer the world with their bare hands, climb mountains with their bare feet, and run longer than any Duracell battery. However, undoubtedly, this concept is not true! The absolute truth is that a man needs lots of support from his woman. Ladies, our men may be physically stronger than us, however, they are mentally, psychologically and emotionally weaker than us. They crave and need our support to operate at their optimal level.

Now support here does not only speak to helping your mate in his quest to define himself or make the family financially stable. Support here also means supporting your man, in any area of his life where help is needed. Sometimes, all it takes is an encouraging note, text or email, buying something for him that he couldn't afford to buy for himself or even buying something to say I am thinking about you and or a hug & kiss to let him feel as if he can conquer the world. It behooves us as wives to provide a substantial amount of support to our men. So that they can matriculate into the individuals that they are yearning to become, and don't worry; if he is really your man, and you are really his woman, then you are at the heart of his plans.

His Blueprint Craves Your Support
Moments of Truth (Be Completely Honest)

Activity 1

Set aside twenty (20) minutes to talk with your husband about his blue print. Spend time helping him to complete his thoughts and visions.

Activity 2

Write down your husbands 'blue print' (goals, visions and dreams)

_____

_____

_____

_____

Activity 3

What can you do to assist him with bringing his plans to reality?

_____
_____
_____
_____
_____
_____
_____
_____
_____
_____
_____
_____
_____
_____

Secret #8

Make Self Love and Care Your First, Priority

As I spent time reading and thinking about the responses from these fifty (50) men, I began to feel a bit overwhelmed. The demands and requirements highlighted, left me feeling a bit insufficient as I looked at 'the man in the mirror.' The truth is that the word 'wife' is just a title. A title that has been given to a woman that has committed herself to be the best companion that she can be. This title of 'wife', is just one of the titles given to a woman that has many hats to fill. She is a wife, a mother, a daughter, a C.E.O, a teacher, a cosmetologist, a friend, an aunt, a cousin, a neighbor, a lover and the list goes on. All of these titles make great demands of her daily. All of these titles require her to operate from a place of excellence.

As women, the world in which we live continuously takes from us and makes its demands. All of these expectations continuously sap our energy and deplete our substance as women. Hence, before we attempt to satisfy our men and save the world in which we live, let us make a conscious commitment to make self-love and care our first priority. Making self-love and care our first priority is the only way that we can execute well and perform at our optimal level. We must become diligent in setting aside the time to care for ourselves mentally, emotionally, physically and spiritually.

Ladies let's not joke about this necessity to love and care for ourselves first, if we do not make selflove and care our first priority, we will become defeated and depleted as women. Hence, it is of utmost importance that we spend the time to care for our minds, by feeding it with healthy and holistic thoughts. It is necessary that we also care for our emotions by being kind, tenderhearted, compassionate, forgiving and loving to ourselves. It is also of equal importance that we take the time to care for our bodies as well. And ladies, do I need to reiterate what all the experts say about the importance of eating healthy and exercising regularly? No, I don't! You already know that your chances of success increase exponentially when you discipline yourself to eat healthily and exercise regularly.

You just need to take the first baby steps and make these habits simple and effortless, so that you can be consistent in your endeavors. And reading a book, yes, you heard me correctly. Reading a book is a great place to start! Make reading a habit. Just three (3) pages of reading per day has the potential to change your life. The day I started reading was the day, my life changed for the better in every area of my life. Reading motivational books, autobiographies and memoirs of great people will arm you with the strategies that you need to live your best life. So, take the first steps in making reading a habit today!

Finally, and most importantly, I must highlight the importance of praying and establishing a relationship with God. As a wife, inevitably, you will face various challenges along this marital path. And as such, you will need to rely on God's wisdom, strength and help to navigate these challenges. Praying and establishing a relationship with God is the foundation for all of life's successes. There will be days when you will become frustrated, angry and maybe even irrational. You will be experiencing the battle of your life! Hence, having that spiritual place to rejuvenate and restore your soul is crucial to your success. You will need spiritual help! You will need God's help in riding your storms and conquering the battles in your marriage.

Make Self Love and Care Your First, Priority
Moments of Truth
(Be Completely Honest)

Activity 1

Make prayer and meditation a habit. Select a time in the day when you can pray and meditate for at least ten (10) minutes.

_____

Activity 2

Start a fitness regime! Choose at least three (3) days in each week to exercise for at least ten (10) minutes.

Activity 3

Read a book! Choose a book and read at least three (3) pages of a motivational book, autobiography or memoirs of great men and women.

Here's a great place to start:

    No excuses by Brian Tracy

    The Compound Effect by Darren Hardy

    The Slight Edge by Jeff Olson

    Think and Grow Rich by Napoleon Hill

    Essentialism by Greg Mckeown

    Act Like A Lady Think Like A Man by Steve Harvey

    Kill Fear by Krystal Tomlinson

    Thrive or Survive by Nicole Mclaren Campbell

    Make it Count by Nicole Mclaren Campbell

    Rich Dad Poor Dad by Robert Kiyosaki

    High Performance Habits by Brendon Burchard

Thank You for Reading This Book

Thank you for spending the time to read this book. I pray that you will do the work needed to fortify and heal infidelity in your marriage.

Please leave a review on Amazon

Also, visit my website at www.deciannrichards.com to receive your free workbook on 'Healing Infidelity In Your Marriage'.

Appendix

Actual Questionnaire Used in Research

Infidelity in Marriages

The information derived from this survey will be used to write a book. The author is aware that the issue being queried is very sensitive in nature. Hence this survey is completely anonymous. In that, it does not collect or reveal the email addresses or phone numbers of any respondent.

Hence only your honest answers are required.

N.B Only male respondents are required for this survey.

---

1. What is your current relationship status?

   - Separated
   - Divorced
   - Single
   - Married

2. Have you ever been married?

- Yes

- No

3. If yes, while being married have you ever had a sexually relationship with any female other than your wife?

- Yes

- No

4. If no, have you ever been tempted to have a sexual relationship with any woman other than your wife?

- Yes

- No

5. In your opinion explain what triggered this temptation to commit infidelity?

_____

_____

6. What were the primary factors that prevented you from actually committing infidelity?

_____

_____

7. If you have had sexual relations with another female other than your wife, what was the nature of this relationship?

- One time event

- A sexual relationship that lasted for a while

- A sexual relationship that became a permanent situation

8. What most attracted you to this other female companion?
_____
_____

9. Please describe the primary feeling/s that you experienced while being with this female companion?
_____
_____

10. When you were with her (female companion), what were the top three (3) activities that you engaged in that sustained these feelings?
_____
_____

11. What do you believe kept you going back to this woman?
_____
_____

12. What characteristic/s did you most love about this other woman that you wished your wife had?

_____
_____

13. In your opinion, what do you honestly believe lead to you having a sexual relationship with this other woman?

_____
_____

14. If your wife began to exhibit most or even some of these core qualities that you found in this other female companion, would you recommit yourself to the marital relationship?

- Yes

- No

15. Please explain the reason/s for your response in question 14.

_____
_____

16. If your response is 'no' to question 14, is it that you would prefer being married whilst still having a sexually relationship with the other women?

- Yes   No

END OF QUESTIONAIRRE

References

Chapman, G. D. (2010). *The 5 Love Languages*: The Secret to Love That Lasts. Chicago: Northfield Publishing.

Harvey, S. (2011). *Think Like a Lady Act Like A Man.* New York: HarperCollins Publishers.

Huff Post. (2017). Research Proves Couples That Laugh together Are In It For The Long Haul. Retrieved from https://www.huffingtonpost.ca/2017/02/10/laughtogether-relationship-couples_n_14677638.html

Mayo Clinic. (2019). *Low Sex Drive in Women.* Retrieved from https://www.mayoclinic.org/diseasesc o n d i t i o n s / l o w - s e x - d r i v e - i n women/symptoms-causes/syc-20374554

Price, A. (2018). *How to Increase Libido the Natural Way.* Retrieved from https://draxe.com/health/urological-health/how-to-increase-libido/

Purdue Online Writing Lab (2019). Reference List:

Author/Authors. Retrieved from https://owl.purdue.edu/owl/research_and_citation/apa_style/apa_formatting_and_style_guide/reference _list_author_authors.html

Valli, F.(1975. My Eyes Adored You: Retrieved from
https://www.youtube.com/watch?v=Xqz9eyakGqY

Printed in Great Britain
by Amazon